5/14

mapping AFRICA

Gareth Stevens
Publishing

By Barbara Linde

Please visit our website, www.garethstevens.com. For a free color catalog of all our high-quality books, call toll free 1-800-542-2595 or fax 1-877-542-2596.

Library of Congress Cataloging-in-Publication Data

Linde, Barbara M.
Mapping Africa / Barbara M. Linde.
    pages cm. — (Mapping the world)
Includes index.
ISBN 978-1-4339-9090-8 (pbk.)
ISBN 978-1-4339-9091-5 (6-pack)
ISBN 978-1-4339-9089-2 (library binding)
1. Maps–Africa–Juvenile literature. 2. Africa–Geography–Juvenile literature. 3. Africa–Description and travel–Juvenile literature. I. Title. II. Series: Mapping the world.
GA1341.L56 2013
916—dc23

                              2012049124

First Edition

Published in 2014 by
Gareth Stevens Publishing
111 East 14th Street, Suite 349
New York, NY 10003

Designer: Katelyn E. Reynolds
Editor: Kristen Rajczak

Photo credits: Cover, p. 1 (photo) Galyna Andrushko/Shutterstock.com; cover, pp. 1, 5 (map) Tom Patterson and Eric Gaba/US National Park Service/Wikipedia.com; cover, pp. 1–24 (banner) kanate/Shutterstock.com; cover, pp. 1–24 (series elements and cork background) iStockphoto/Thinkstock.com; pp. 5 (compass rose), 15 (icons), 19 (both), 21 (the Pyramids, the Nile River, Mount Kilimanjaro) iStockphoto/Thinkstock.com; p. 7 Ingram Publishing/Thinkstock.com; p. 9 The World Factbook/CIA; p. 11 (main) AridOcean/Shutterstock.com; p. 11 (inset) Digital Vision/Thinkstock.com; p. 13 (main) Roberto Caucino/Shutterstock.com; p. 13 (inset) Ingoman/Wikipedia.com; pp. 15 (map), 17 (inset map) Miguel Contreras, Guatemala/Wikipedia.com; p. 17 (main) PIUS UTOMI EKPEI/AFP/Getty Images; p. 21 (Kruger National Park) Natursports/Shutterstock.com; p. 21 (Victoria Falls) Paul Murtagh/Shutterstock.com; p. 21 (Kimberley Diamond Mines) Selwyn Tait/Time Life Pictures/Getty Images; p. 21 (map) dalmingo/Shutterstock.com.

Printed in the United States of America

CPSIA compliance information: Batch #CS13GS: For further information contact Gareth Stevens, New York, New York at 1-800-542-2595.

CONTENTS

Words in the glossary appear in **bold** type the first time they are used in the text.

WELCOME TO AFRICA

Africa is the second-largest **continent** in the world. It's about 5,200 miles (8,370 km) long from north to south. The Atlantic Ocean lies to the west. The Indian Ocean lies to the east. These two oceans meet to form Africa's southern border. The Mediterranean Sea lies to the north.

Look at the compass rose on the map on page 5. It shows you the four cardinal directions: north, south, east, and west. When you know the directions, you can locate any point on Earth.

Where in the World?

Africa is almost three times as large as the United States.

4

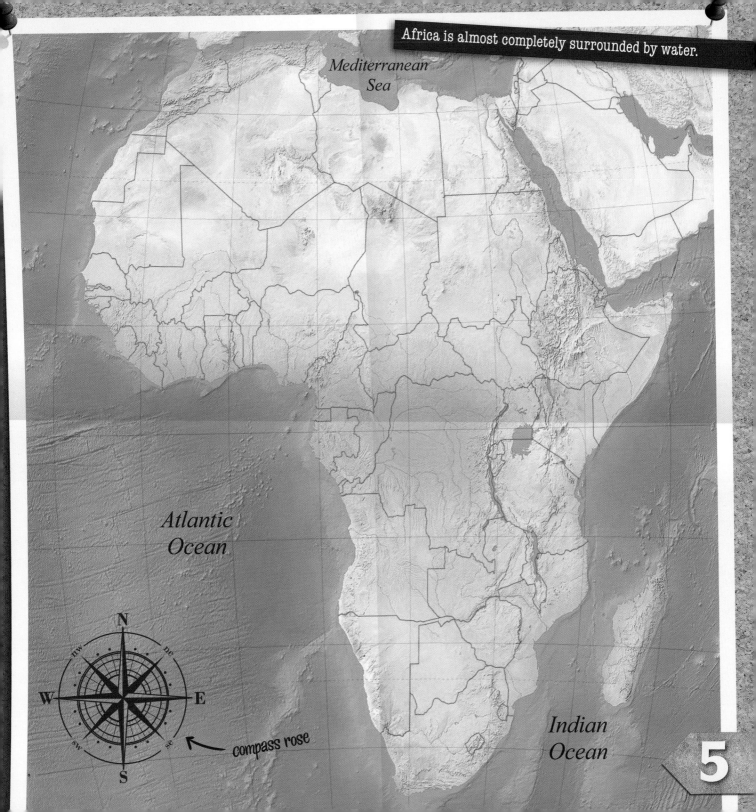

Africa is almost completely surrounded by water.

Mediterranean Sea

Atlantic Ocean

Indian Ocean

N
nw   ne
W   E
sw   se
S

compass rose

5

WHERE IN THE WORLD IS AFRICA?

The equator is an imaginary line that runs around the middle of Earth. It divides Earth into Northern and Southern **Hemispheres**. Over half of Africa is above the equator, so it's in the Northern Hemisphere. The area below the equator is in the Southern Hemisphere.

The Prime Meridian is an imaginary line that runs from north to south. It divides Earth into Eastern and Western Hemispheres. Most of Africa is in the Eastern Hemisphere. A small part of it is in the Western Hemisphere.

Where in the World?

The imaginary lines that run east and west above and below the equator are called lines of latitude. The imaginary lines that run north and south on either side of the Prime Meridian are called lines of longitude.

6

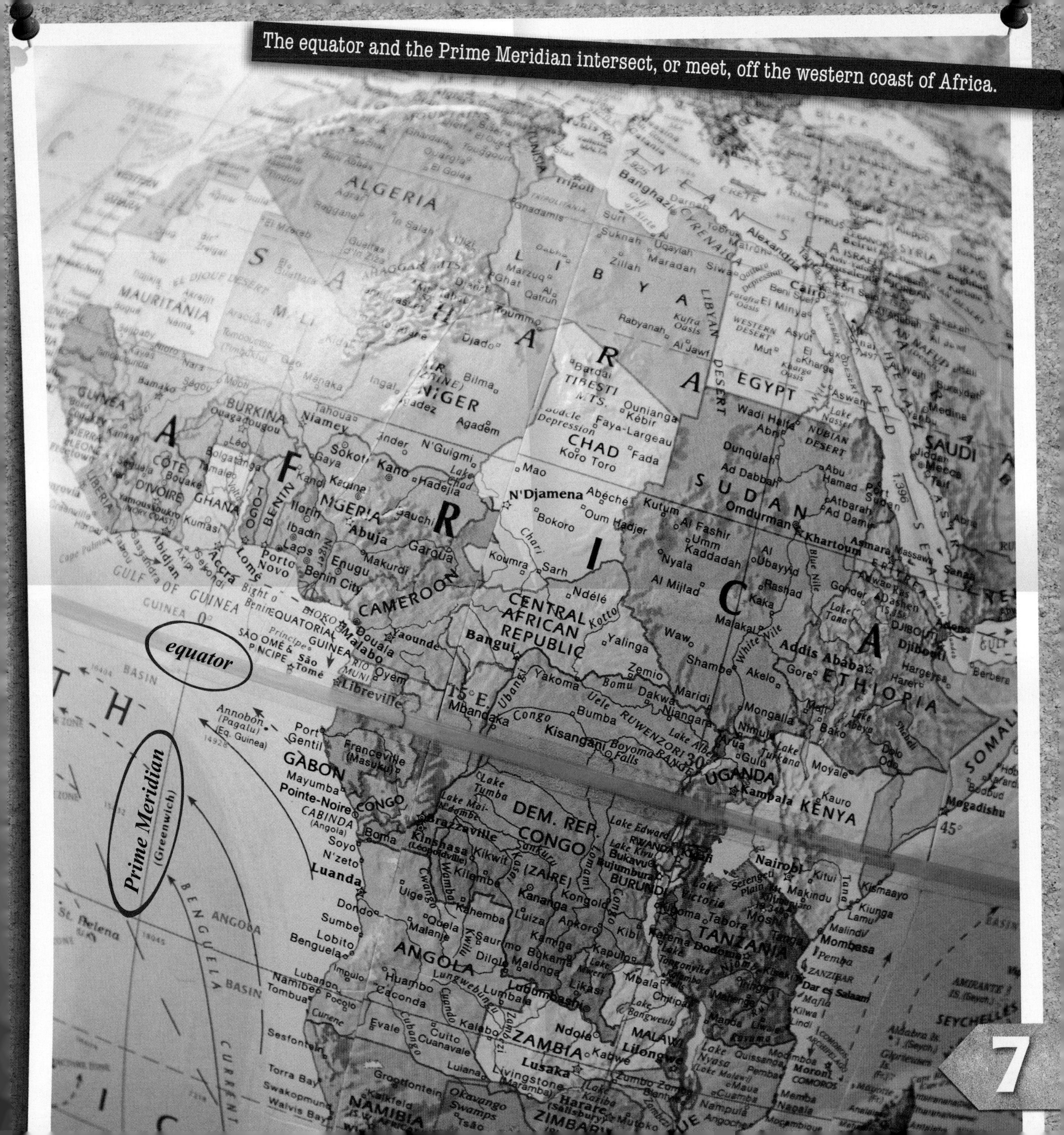

The equator and the Prime Meridian intersect, or meet, off the western coast of Africa.

THE COUNTRIES OF AFRICA

Africa has 53 countries that are recognized by the **African Union**, or AU. A **political** map shows the **boundaries** for each country. Landforms are often used as political boundaries. The border between two countries also can be a place that one or both of the countries choose.

Find the country of Egypt on the map. The Mediterranean and the Red Sea are two of its boundaries. Lines on the map also show its borders with the countries of Libya and Sudan.

Where in the World?

The name of a country might change when the government changes. The country of Ethiopia was once called Abyssinia. Together, Burundi, Rwanda, and Tanzania used to be known as German East Africa.

8

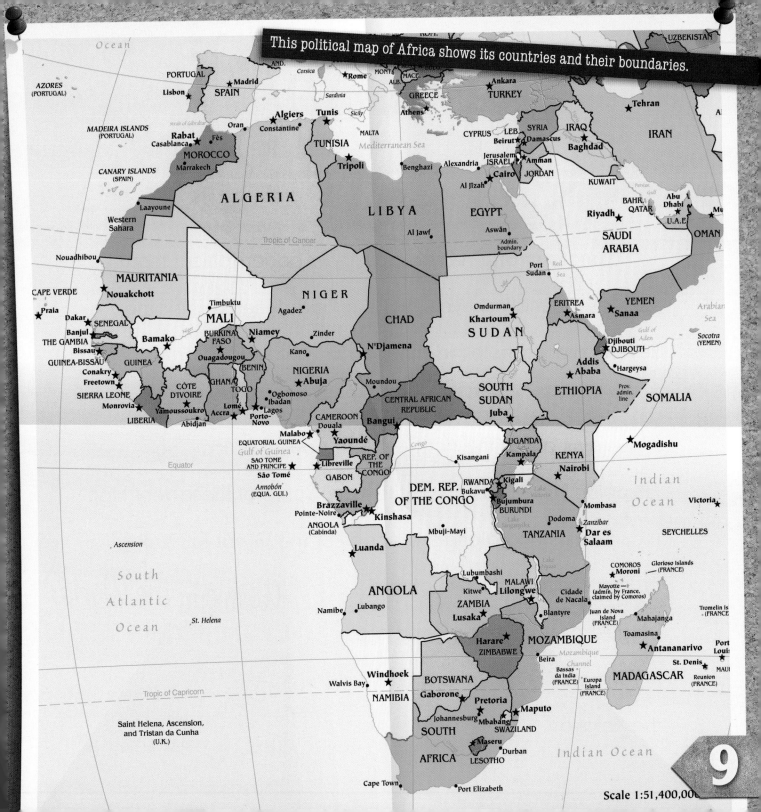

This political map of Africa shows its countries and their boundaries.

9

Scale 1:51,400,000

THE LANDFORMS OF AFRICA

Landform and relief maps show geographical features, such as mountains, rivers, valleys, and deserts. Their map key or coloring helps **identify** each type of landform.

Look at all the mountain ranges in Africa! The Atlas Mountains are in the northwestern part of Africa. The Ethiopian Highlands are in the east. Some of these very high mountains stand along the edges of the Great Rift Valley, or East African Rift. Two of the biggest deserts in the world are in Africa, too—the Sahara and the Kalahari.

Where in the World?

Eighty percent of the tallest mountains in Africa are found in the Ethiopian Highlands. Some of the mountains there are more than 14,000 feet (4,267 m) high!

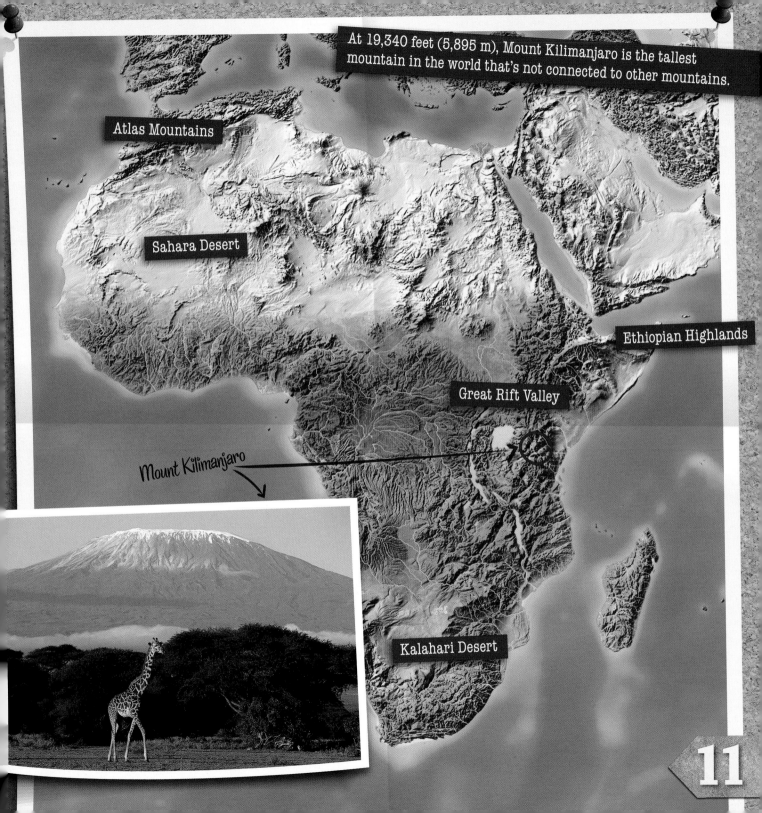

At 19,340 feet (5,895 m), Mount Kilimanjaro is the tallest mountain in the world that's not connected to other mountains.

Atlas Mountains

Sahara Desert

Ethiopian Highlands

Great Rift Valley

Mount Kilimanjaro

Kalahari Desert

THE CLIMATES OF AFRICA

Climate is the temperature and weather of a place over a long period of time. The climate affects the number of people who live in an area. It also affects the kinds of plants and animals found there.

The continent of Africa is so big, it has many different climates. Rainforests occur in the **tropical**, wet climate zones. Deserts are found in the **arid** climates. Areas near the coasts have mild but wet, or humid, climates.

Where in the World?

The climate of a place depends on how far it is from the equator. The hottest climates are closest to the equator. The coldest are the farthest away.

Sahara Desert

forestland

savanna

grassland

semidesert

extreme desert

Africa Climate Map

The Sahara Desert is the world's largest hot desert. It's the large arid area in northern Africa.

13

THE RESOURCES OF AFRICA

Africa has many **natural resources**. A map like this one shows what the resources are and where to find them. Bananas, coffee, cocoa, and rubber trees are all grown in Africa. **Mining** and farming the natural resources give jobs to millions of people.

Mineral resources include oil and gas. Iron and copper are found in several places. Some of the largest diamond and gold mines on Earth are in South Africa. The country is full of agricultural—or farming—resources, too.

Where in the World?

Many people from all over Africa come to South Africa to work in the mines, farms, and factories.

14

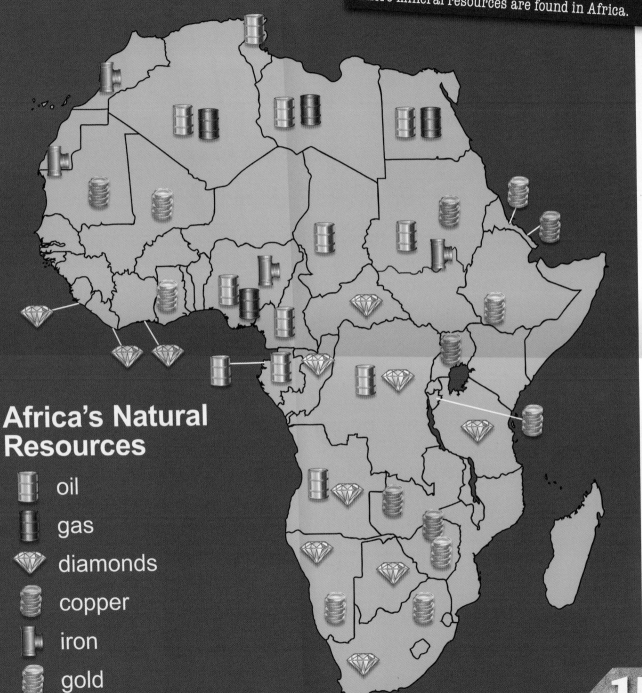

This natural resources map can help you see where mineral resources are found in Africa.

Africa's Natural Resources

- oil
- gas
- diamonds
- copper
- iron
- gold

15

THE POPULATION OF AFRICA

There are about 1 billion people living in Africa. A population map shows where they live. The map key has different colors. These colors show the number of people who live in a square kilometer. Most people live near rivers or lakes, or along the coasts.

In Africa, some people live in large, crowded cities such as Lagos, Nigeria. Others live in smaller towns. Still others live in tiny villages. A small number of people raise animals and travel from place to place with their animals.

Where in the World?

Nigeria has the most people of any country in Africa. About 170 million people live there. The island country of Seychelles has the smallest number of people. Only about 90,000 people live there.

16

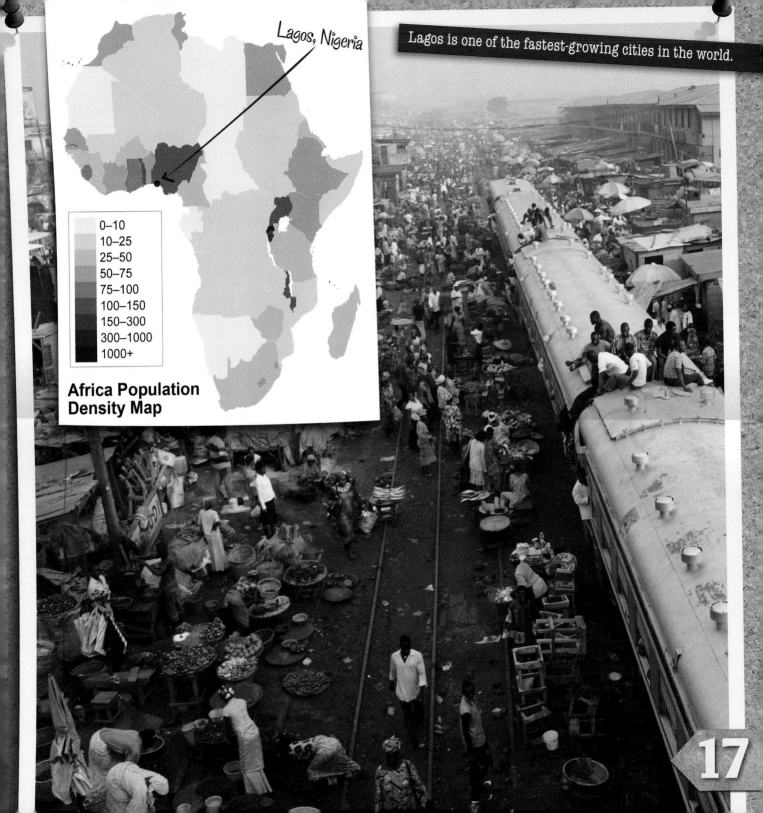

Lagos, Nigeria

Africa Population Density Map

0–10
10–25
25–50
50–75
75–100
100–150
150–300
300–1000
1000+

Lagos is one of the fastest-growing cities in the world.

17

THE CITIES OF AFRICA

Many countries in Africa have small and large cities. On a map, capital cities are often shown with a star. Large cities are shown by large dots. Smaller cities are shown with smaller dots.

Cairo is the capital of Egypt and is one of the largest cities in Africa. Almost 11 million people live there. South Africa has three capital cities: Pretoria, Cape Town, and Bloemfontein. Maseru is the capital of Lesotho, a tiny African country that has a population of only 1.9 million.

Where in the World?

The city of Cairo is more than 1,000 years old. The Nile River runs through the city.

Though there are many historic places to visit in Cairo, parts of the city are very modern, too.

THE LANDMARKS OF AFRICA

There are many exciting landmarks to visit in Africa. The pyramids in Egypt are some of the most famous landmarks in the world! They were built more than 4,000 years ago.

Tourists often take **safaris** through Kruger National Park in South Africa. Do you want to see an awesome water show? Visit Victoria Falls, located on the Zambezi River between Zambia and Zimbabwe. Kimberley Diamond Mine in South Africa is the largest diamond mine in the world.

Where in the World?

Victoria Falls is also known as Mosi-oa-Tunya, which means the "smoke that thunders."

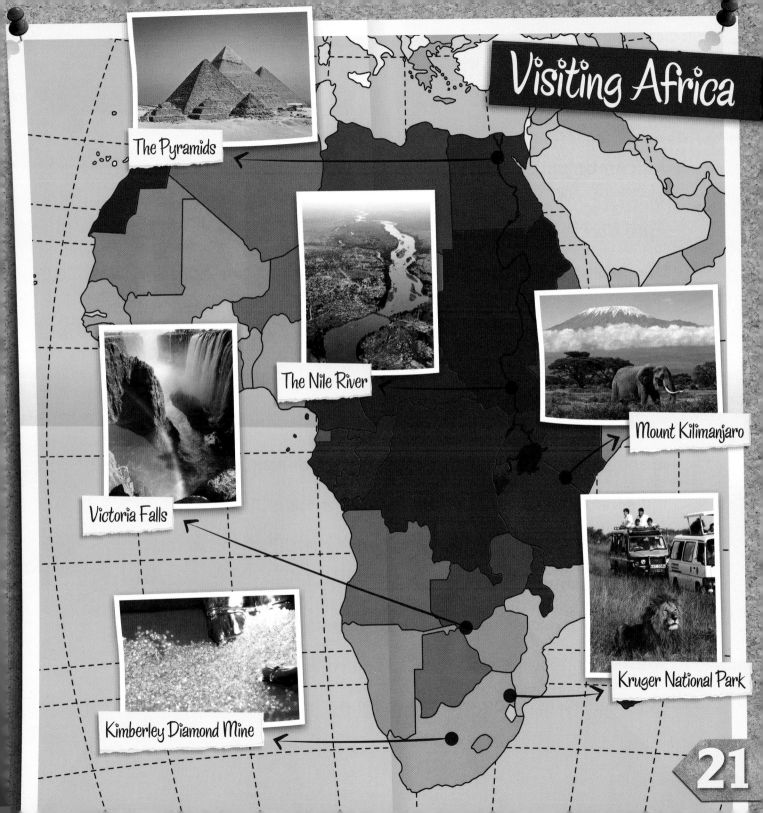

Visiting Africa

The Pyramids

The Nile River

Mount Kilimanjaro

Victoria Falls

Kruger National Park

Kimberley Diamond Mine

21

GLOSSARY

African Union: a group of African countries that work together to make the continent more peaceful and successful

arid: dry

boundary: the line, fence, landform, or other object that separates one country from another

continent: one of the seven large landmasses on Earth. They are Asia, Africa, Europe, North America, South America, Australia, and Antarctica.

hemisphere: one-half of Earth

identify: to find out the name or features of something

mineral: matter in the ground that forms rocks

mining: the act of digging up minerals and other resources

natural resource: something in nature that can be used by people

political: having to do with the government

safari: a trip, usually in Africa, to see wild animals.

tropical: having to do with the warm parts of Earth near the equator

FOR MORE INFORMATION

Books

Croze, Harvey. *Africa for Kids: Exploring a Vibrant Continent, 19 Activities.* Chicago, IL: Chicago Review Press, 2006.

Friedman, Mel. *Africa.* New York, NY: Children's Press, 2009.

Websites

Africa
www.pbs.org/wnet/africa/
Use this website to explore the continent of Africa and its many countries.

Africa
www.africa.mrdonn.org/
Use this website to learn more about the geography, history, and cultures of Africa.

South Africa
kids.nationalgeographic.com/kids/places/find/south-africa/
Read facts and view photos of South Africa.

INDEX